A Pillar Box Red Publication

in association with

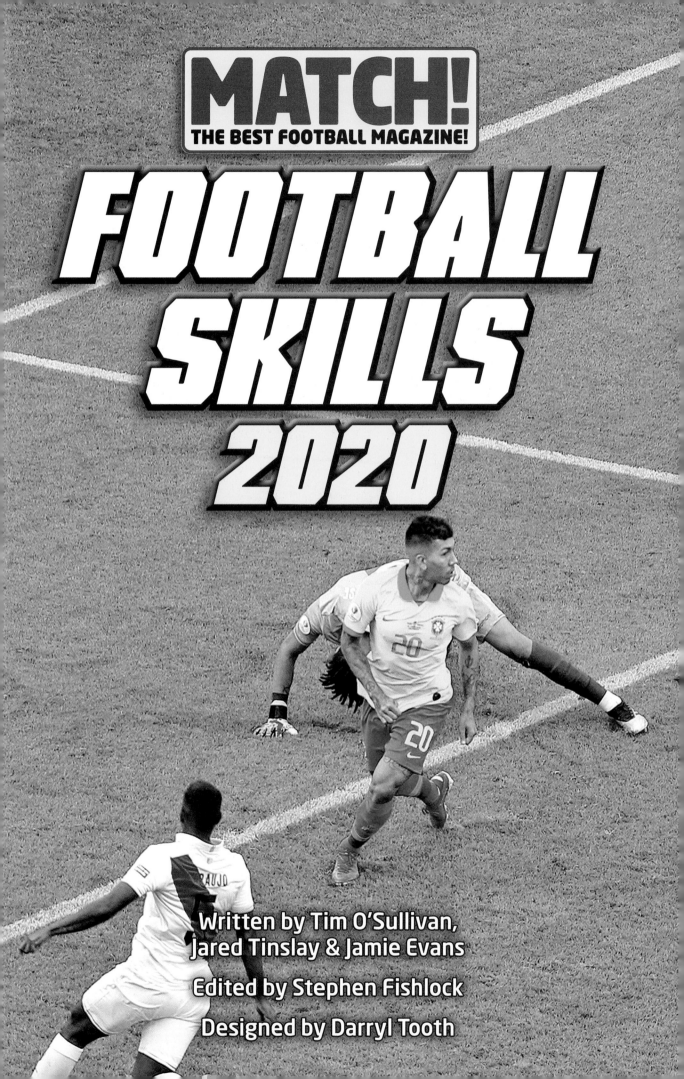

FOOTBALL SKILLS 2020

Written by Tim O'Sullivan,
Jared Tinslay & Jamie Evans

Edited by Stephen Fishlock

Designed by Darryl Tooth

CONTENTS

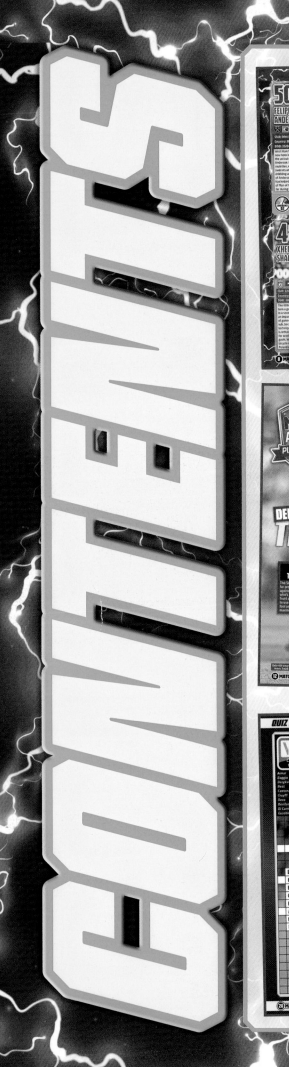

ROBERTO FIRMINO
PULL SPIN STEP OVER!

PLAY LIKE FIRMINO 54

FIFA SKILLS

Try out some of these mega simple skills on EA SPORTS' FIFA!

FIFA SKILLS 14, 22, 36 & 46

ANGEL DI MARIA
THE HIGH WAVE!

PLAY LIKE DI MARIA 38

50

FELIPE ANDERSON

Club: West Ham
Country: Brazil
DOB: 15/04/93

West Ham fans bagged a new hero in 2018-19 with the arrival of Felipe Anderson. Flip-flaps, roulettes, epic body swerves and dynamite dribbling are all part of Anderson's skill set, which has helped him pick up loads of Man of the Match awards so far during his West Ham career!

CONFIDENCE	DRIBBLING	TRICKS	AGILITY	WEAK FOOT
82	85	79	77	78

49

JULIAN DRAXLER

Club: PSG
Country: Germany
DOB: 20/09/93

Draxler is one of the trickiest footy stars on the planet! He's struggled to showcase his talents at PSG, which isn't surprising when a superstar like Kylian Mbappe is your team-mate, but he was still a big part of their Ligue 1 success in 2018-19 by mesmerising supporters with his ace skills!

CONFIDENCE	DRIBBLING	TRICKS	AGILITY	WEAK FOOT
77	83	86	76	95

48

XHERDAN SHAQIRI

Club: Liverpool
Country: Switzerland
DOB: 10/10/91

The little Swiss genius can turn a game upside down in a second! He can make an impact from the start of games or as a super sub, because his mix of technique and close control is lethal. He's also famous for scoring jaw-dropping goals, including his sick bicycle-kick against Poland at Euro 2016!

TOP SKILL!
THE SLAP CUT!

CONFIDENCE	DRIBBLING	TRICKS	AGILITY	WEAK FOOT
85	84	80	70	82

47

MOHAMED SALAH

Club: *Liverpool*
Country: *Egypt*
DOB: 15/06/92

Liverpool's Egyptian king bosses Anfield with his electric pace, sensational body feints, slick dribbling and lethal finishing! Salah was an exciting talent when he was at Roma, but now he's a global superstar known all over the world. What a total legend!

TOP SKILL!
THE FLIP FLAP!

CONFIDENCE	DRIBBLING	TRICKS	AGILITY	WEAK FOOT
96	94	74	93	88

46

JAMES MADDISON

Club: *Leicester*
Country: *England*
DOB: 23/11/96

Maddison had spells at Coventry and Norwich before sealing a big Prem move to Leicester in 2018. He made an instant impact with a top-quality performance against Man. United at Old Trafford, and hasn't looked back since. His creativity and free-kick technique are absolutely awesome!

45

GELSON MARTINS

Club: *Monaco*
Country: *Portugal*
DOB: 11/05/95

Martins has already played for European giants Sporting, Atletico Madrid and Monaco in his career before the age of 25! He has the potential to be top ten in this list in future years, because when he's on top of his game the Portugal speedster's tricky wing play is out of this world!

CONFIDENCE	DRIBBLING	TRICKS	AGILITY	WEAK FOOT
93	77	77	76	84

CONFIDENCE	DRIBBLING	TRICKS	AGILITY	WEAK FOOT
71	83	85	78	71

44
JAMES RODRIGUEZ

Club: *Real Madrid*
Country: *Colombia*
DOB: *12/07/91*

So many footy stars have awesome athleticism or raw power, but James Rodriguez is all about old-school technique. The way he executes tricky volleys, scooped passes and long-range curlers prove the Colombia legend is one of the most skilful footy heroes on the planet!

CONFIDENCE	DRIBBLING	TRICKS	AGILITY	WEAK FOOT
81	79	80	77	80

43
LORENZO INSIGNE

Club: *Napoli*
Country: *Italy*
DOB: *04/06/91*

Most of the greatest stars in Italian footy history are keepers or defenders, but now and again an attacking talent makes a mark in the famous country. Insigne has been compared to Italy legend Roberto Baggio for his wicked mixture of flair, creativity, aggression and dribbling!

CONFIDENCE	DRIBBLING	TRICKS	AGILITY	WEAK FOOT
83	83	80	79	76

42
THIAGO ALCANTARA

Club: *Bayern Munich*
Country: *Spain*
DOB: *11/04/91*

We can't get enough of Thiago – he's everything you'd want from a central midfielder! He can get stuck in, plays pinpoint long or short passes and be creative. But we love him because he adds dribbling, tricks and flair to all the boring stuff. Opposition midfielders just can't handle his mega quick thinking!

CONFIDENCE	DRIBBLING	TRICKS	AGILITY	WEAK FOOT
88	83	80	77	88

41
WILLIAN

Club: *Chelsea*
Country: *Brazil*
DOB: *09/08/88*

Willian spends a lot of time on the bench for Chelsea and Brazil, but we can't work out why he doesn't start more games. He's so cool and controlled in possession, has close-control skills as good as anyone on the footy planet and busts out some legendary tricks and free-kicks!

CONFIDENCE	DRIBBLING	TRICKS	AGILITY	WEAK FOOT
72	82	84	73	80

40

PAULO DYBALA

Club: *Juventus*
Country: *Argentina*
DOB: *15/11/93*

The tricky Argentina ace is more than just a goal grabber. He can escape man-markers with his slick turns, cheeky nutmegs and rapid one-twos! Dybala's link-up play with Juve team-mates Cristiano Ronaldo and Miralem Pjanic totally bosses Serie A. Nobody in Italy can stop them!

CONFIDENCE
88

DRIBBLING
81

TRICKS
80

AGILITY
80

WEAK FOOT
81

MATCH! ACADEMY
Play like the stars!

DELE ALLI
THE SLAP CUT!

SHIELD THE BALL!

The Slap Cut is perfect for protecting possession against an opponent who's to the side or in front of you. Make sure to use your furthest foot and upper body for maximum protection!

THESE SKILLS HELP YOU...

Create chances for yourself and team-mates! ✓

Change direction and shield the ball! ✓

Be unpredictable in 1 v 1 situations! ✓

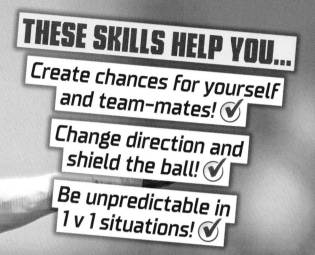

CREATE SCORING CHANCES!

Deadly England and Tottenham midfielder Dele Alli loves doing this skill when he's travelling across goal. It helps him create space for a shot or to play a killer pass to a team-mate!

CHANGE DIRECTION!

If you don't have space to run, shoot or pass, use the Slap Cut to shield the ball and change direction quickly. Watch out for Dele busting this out loads for Spurs in the Prem this season!

TRAINING GROUND!
Now practise the skill yourself!

STEP 1

Push the ball forward and roll the inside of your right foot over the ball, then stop it with the outside of the same foot.

STEP 2

Quickly change direction and direct the ball forwards with your right foot.

STEP 3

Finally, accelerate away with the ball. Then repeat with your left foot to master the skill with both feet!

NOW WATCH THE VIDEOS!

Go to the MATCH website to see how to do the Slap Cut, plus check out loads more cool ball mastery and mirror move videos linked to this skill...

INSIDE OUTSIDE ROLL

SLAP CUT STEP OVER

www.matchfootball.co.uk

FIFA SKILLS

Try out some of these mega simple skills on EA SPORTS' FIFA!

TOP TIPS!

When you see an arrow pointing upwards, that means flick or hold the right or left stick the way that your player is facing, while the down arrow is behind you!

You don't have to learn every single one of these tricks off by heart. Master one or two first, then add the others to your arsenal one by one!

Go to player info to check out your players' skill rating. Five-star skillers can do every trick in the book, but one-star skillers can only do the basics!

CHOP ★★★★

Quickly change direction while running at speed!

HOLD: L2/LT   **TAP:** Circle/B + Cross/A

L2 / LT   ● / B + ✕ / A

1

2

DRAG BACK ★★

Roll the ball under your foot using your sole, then quickly turn around!

HOLD: R1/RB + L Stick Down

R1 / RB + L ↓

1

2

BALL ROLL ★★

Shift the ball from one side to the other using the sole of your boot!

HOLD: R Stick Left **OR HOLD:** R Stick Right

R ←   R →

NO TOUCH ★

Keep your opponent guessing without touching the ball!

HOLD: R1/RB

R1 / RB

STEPOVER ★★

Push the right stick forward and to the side to pull out this classic move!

ROTATE: R Stick Up, Right **OR ROTATE:** R Stick Up, Left

R ↱   R ↰

39
RICHARLISON

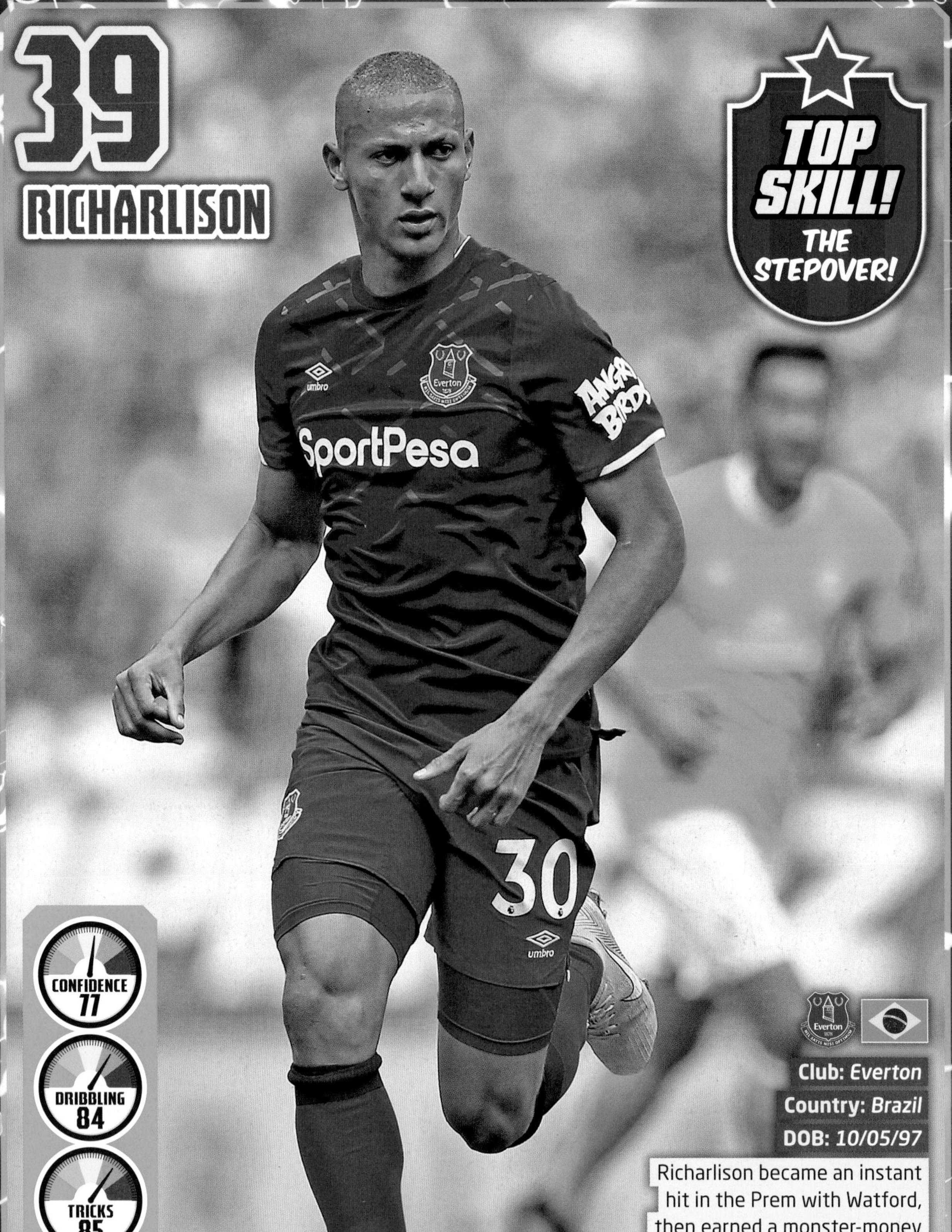

TOP SKILL!

THE STEPOVER!

CONFIDENCE
77

DRIBBLING
84

TRICKS
85

AGILITY
80

WEAK FOOT
73

Club: Everton
Country: Brazil
DOB: 10/05/97

Richarlison became an instant hit in the Prem with Watford, then earned a monster-money move to Everton! His changes of pace and stepovers have been tough for Prem defenders to stop since he flew over from Fluminense in Brazil in 2017. His Samba skills are too good!

38 DELE ALLI

Club: Tottenham
Country: England
DOB: 11/04/96

Dele's famous for his clever movement, accurate headers and class passing, but he's also a trickster! He stunned the crowd with an epic roulette and body feint against Man. City last season, and he loves a nutmeg too – even against his team-mates in training!

CONFIDENCE	DRIBBLING	TRICKS	AGILITY	WEAK FOOT
91	75	84	81	83

37 DUSAN TADIC

Club: Ajax
Country: Serbia
DOB: 20/11/88

Southampton supporters rubbed their eyes in disbelief last season, because their former playmaker Dusan Tadic turned into one of Europe's most talked-about stars. His roulettes, stepovers and clever passes stunned Real Madrid and Juventus in the Champions League!

CONFIDENCE	DRIBBLING	TRICKS	AGILITY	WEAK FOOT
87	80	89	71	80

TOP SKILL!
THE BACKHEEL!

36 STEPHAN EL SHAARAWY

Club: Shanghai Greenland Shenhua
Country: Italy
DOB: 27/10/92

El Shaarawy hasn't developed into the global star everyone predicted he would become when he was a wonderkid, but he's still had a decent career full of dynamite dribbling and sick tricks! The ex-Roma winger has electric pace and turns full-backs inside out. Hero!

CONFIDENCE	DRIBBLING	TRICKS	AGILITY	WEAK FOOT
72	83	88	83	78

35

BERNARDO SILVA

Club: Man. City
Country: Portugal
DOB: 10/08/94

The City genius was one of the best players in the Premier League in 2018-19. Bernardo Silva has been praised for his energy and work-rate, but he's still got the dribbling skills that made him a star at Monaco. He escapes his opponents with unreal close control and slick 360 turns!

CONFIDENCE	DRIBBLING	TRICKS	AGILITY	WEAK FOOT
86	86	81	85	96

34

MARLOS

Club: Shakhtar Donetsk
Country: Ukraine
DOB: 07/06/88

Marlos joins a long list of silky Brazilian-born footy stars with bags of tricks and flair. The 31-year-old plays international footy for the Ukraine now after seven years in the country, but he's still got classic Samba flair. He nutmegs defenders for fun and loves a stepover!

CONFIDENCE	DRIBBLING	TRICKS	AGILITY	WEAK FOOT
83	85	88	80	76

33

LEROY SANE

Club: Man. City
Country: Germany
DOB: 11/01/96

Sane is one of the best wingers we've ever seen in the Premier League. His electric pace terrifies full-backs and he can score goals from any angle. Leroy doesn't bust out jaw-dropping rainbow flicks like Neymar, but his set of skills have a similar impact, with epic changes of pace and body swerves!

TOP SKILL!
THE DRAG PUSH!

CONFIDENCE	DRIBBLING	TRICKS	AGILITY	WEAK FOOT
73	97	85	92	77

TOP SKILL!
NO-LOOK GOAL!

32
ROBERTO FIRMINO

Club: *Liverpool*
Country: *Brazil*
DOB: 02/10/91

Firmino is a hero at Anfield for his incredible work-rate and unselfish team play, but he's also a skilful genius with the ball at his feet. He's most famous for his 'no-look goals', which he's scored for both Liverpool and Brazil, while his flicks and creativity helped Sadio Mane and Mohamed Salah share the 2018-19 Prem Golden Boot!

CONFIDENCE	DRIBBLING	TRICKS	AGILITY	WEAK FOOT
88	80	85	81	88

31
MESUT OZIL

Club: *Arsenal*
Country: *Germany*
DOB: 15/10/88

Ozil has an army of critics, but nobody can deny he's a joy to watch on top form. He became famous at Arsenal for scoring goals with a unique shooting technique, where he'd strike the ball into the ground and make it pop up and bounce over diving goalkeepers. His flicks and backheels rule too!

CONFIDENCE	DRIBBLING	TRICKS	AGILITY	WEAK FOOT
72	85	88	87	83

30
ISCO

Club: *Real Madrid*
Country: *Spain*
DOB: 21/04/92

Isco plays football like it's in slow motion – he looks like he's got all the time in the world and can find space other midfielders can't! He leaves defensive midfielders tackling thin air with his clever 360 turns, roulettes, backheels and chipped passes. His genius can be the difference for Real Madrid and Spain!

CONFIDENCE	DRIBBLING	TRICKS	AGILITY	WEAK FOOT
91	91	87	82	88

WORDFIT

Can you fit these legendary all-time trick machines into this giant grid?

Aimar
Baggio
Bergkamp
Best
Cantona
Cruyff
Deco
Denilson
Di Canio
Eusebio

Figo
Garrincha
Ginola
Kaka
Maradona
Meazza
Okocha
Ortega
Pele
Prosinecki

Puskas
Riquelme
Rivaldo
Robinho
Ronaldinho
Ronaldo
Waddle
Zico
Zidane
Zola

5 QUESTIONS ON...
RICHARLISON

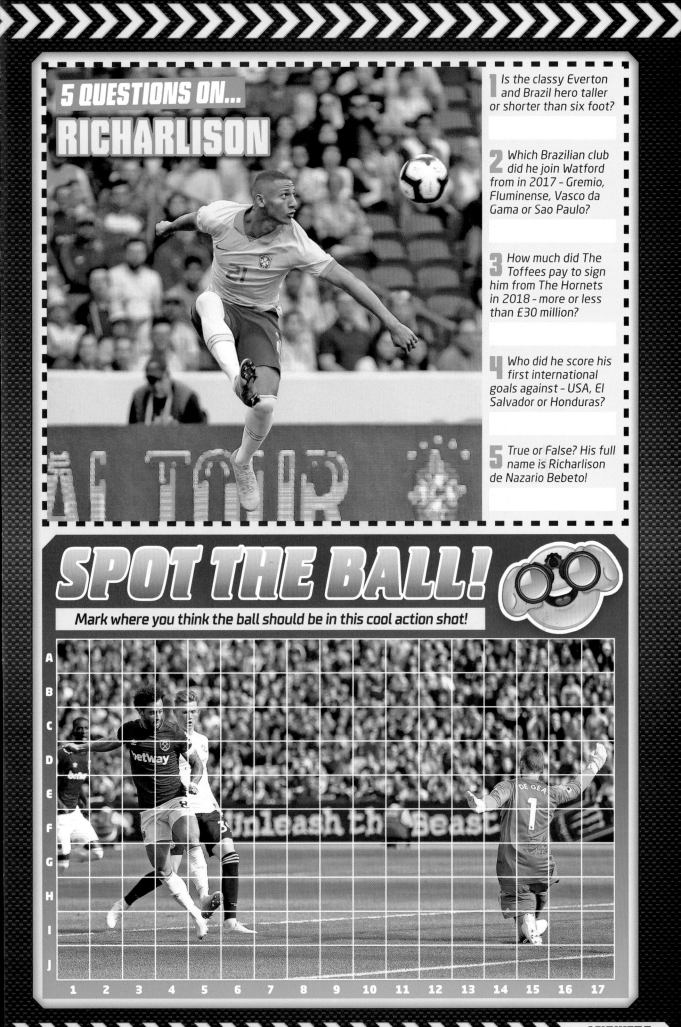

1 Is the classy Everton and Brazil hero taller or shorter than six foot?

2 Which Brazilian club did he join Watford from in 2017 - Gremio, Fluminense, Vasco da Gama or Sao Paulo?

3 How much did The Toffees pay to sign him from The Hornets in 2018 - more or less than £30 million?

4 Who did he score his first international goals against - USA, El Salvador or Honduras?

5 True or False? His full name is Richarlison de Nazario Bebeto!

SPOT THE BALL!

Mark where you think the ball should be in this cool action shot!

ANSWERS ON PAGE 60

FIFA SKILLS

You'll totally tie defenders in knots with these FIFA skill moves!

FAKE SHOT ★

Line up a shot at goal, then fool your opponent by pulling out a dummy!

TAP: Circle/B + Cross/A

⊙ / ⊙ + X / A

1

2

HEEL FLICK ★★★

Get this move right, and defenders won't stand a chance against you!

FLICK:	**THEN FLICK:**
R Stick Up	R Stick Down
R ⬆	R ⬇

1

2

BALL ROLL CUT ★★★★

Add an extra bit of flair to the basic two-star Ball Roll move!

HOLD:
R Stick Left
then
R Stick Right

OR HOLD:
R Stick Right
then
R Stick Left

R ←
R →

R →
R ←

1

2

ROULETTE ★★★

Bring back Zinedine Zidane's world-famous spinning move!

ROTATE:
R Stick 270°

OR ROTATE:
R Stick 270°

R
↓
←
↑
→

R
↓
→
↑
←

1

2

LA CROQUETA ★★★★

This is another four-star version of the Ball Roll - quickly shift the ball from one side to the other!

HOLD: L1/LB + R Stick Left

L1 / LB + R ←

OR HOLD: L1/LB + R Stick Right

L1 / LB + R →

1

2

FLICK UP ★

The move is also known as 'Flick Up For Volley', so after flicking the ball in the air, strike it on the volley!

PRESS:
R Stick

R

1

2

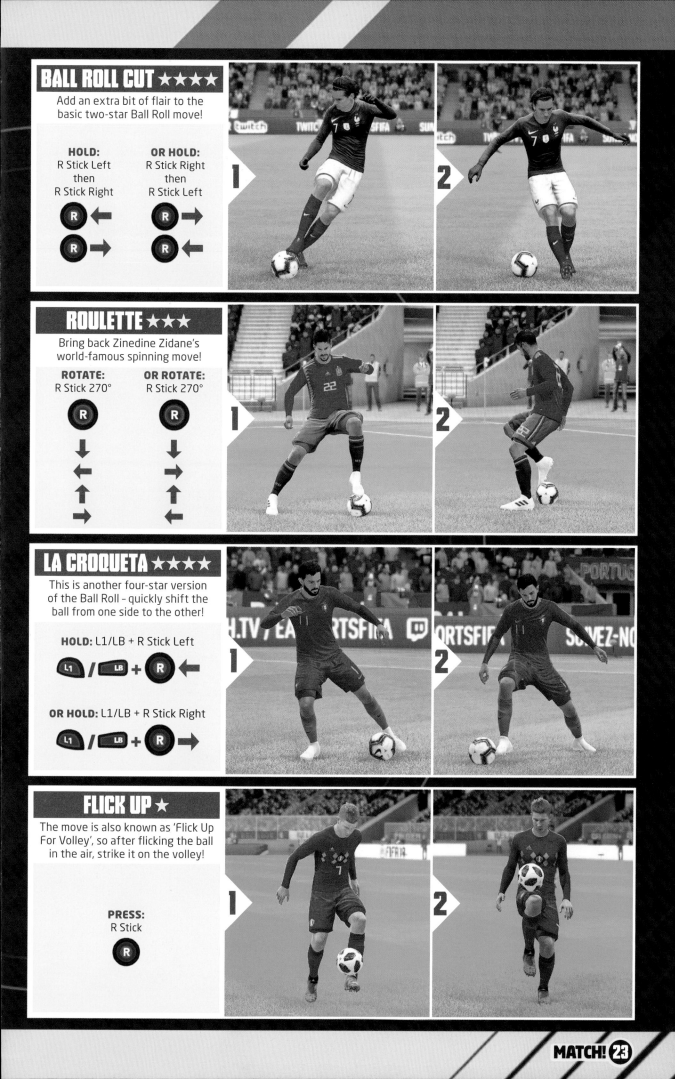

29
HATEM BEN ARFA

Club: *Free Agent*
Country: *France*
DOB: 07/03/87

Ben Arfa has had ups and downs during his career, making him one of the most controversial footy stars in recent years. It might sound crazy, but the only other modern player who bamboozles defenders with dribbling skills like him is Messi!

CONFIDENCE	DRIBBLING	TRICKS	AGILITY	WEAK FOOT
69	98	90	79	73

28
FRENKIE DE JONG

Club: *Barcelona*
Country: *Netherlands*
DOB: 12/05/97

Frenkie became an overnight superstar and earned a big-money move to Barcelona after a life-changing season in 2018-19. Loads of Ajax players became big stars last season, but de Jong had that extra X-factor. His special two-touch move to escape midfielders became a phenomenon on Twitter!

CONFIDENCE	DRIBBLING	TRICKS	AGILITY	WEAK FOOT
90	87	87	86	88

27
PHILIPPE COUTINHO

Club: *Bayern Munich*
Country: *Brazil*
DOB: 12/06/92

Coutinho is the king of the nutmeg! Midfielders always get too close to the classy Brazilian, and he punishes them with a flick around the corner or through their legs. His dribbling is also world class and he can bust out powerful long shots better than most players on the planet!

TOP SKILL!
THE NUTMEG!

CONFIDENCE	DRIBBLING	TRICKS	AGILITY	WEAK FOOT
83	89	88	87	89

26
DIMITRI PAYET

Club: Marseille
Country: France
DOB: 29/03/87

Look away now, West Ham supporters – your former hero is still a big part of our top 50 list! Payet has never had amazing pace, but his footy brain and incredible control help him dribble past defenders like they're not there. He's also curled home some of the craziest free-kicks in footy history!

CONFIDENCE	DRIBBLING	TRICKS	AGILITY	WEAK FOOT
83	95	86	78	88

25
YANNICK BOLASIE

Club: Sporting
Country: DR Congo
DOB: 24/05/89

We're desperate to see more of Bolasie in 2020, because he's still one of the most attacking talents we've seen in the Prem over the past ten years. Some critics question his crossing and finishing, but there's no denying his ability to totally destroy full-backs with eye-popping tricks!

CONFIDENCE	DRIBBLING	TRICKS	AGILITY	WEAK FOOT
85	91	98	82	73

24
HOUSSEM AOUAR

Club: Lyon
Country: France
DOB: 30/06/98

Lyon will do well to keep Aouar at the club long-term, because his rise to footy stardom looks guaranteed. He had a breakout season in 2018-19, helping Lyon finish third in Ligue 1 with a series of Man of the Match displays. His body swerves and clever passing ruin opponents!

CONFIDENCE	DRIBBLING	TRICKS	AGILITY	WEAK FOOT
89	88	86	92	95

23
NANI

Club: *Orlando City*
Country: *Portugal*
DOB: *17/11/86*

Nani's wicked career in European footy has come to an end, but he's still giving defenders nightmares in America with Orlando City! His elite chops, rabonas and stepovers are legendary at some of his former clubs, including Man. United! On top form, he can still destroy even the best full-backs for fun!

CONFIDENCE	DRIBBLING	TRICKS	AGILITY	WEAK FOOT
94	87	96	80	82

22
ANGEL DI MARIA

Club: *PSG*
Country: *Argentina*
DOB: *14/02/88*

Angel Di Maria was born on Valentine's Day and quickly fell in love with football. He simply refuses to play the game in a simple or boring style. PSG's creative king loves finding their lethal strikers with throughballs, backheels and scooped passes. The Argentina ace is a genius!

CONFIDENCE	DRIBBLING	TRICKS	AGILITY	WEAK FOOT
90	88	88	84	89

21
JUAN CUADRADO

Club: *Juventus*
Country: *Colombia*
DOB: *26/05/88*

The legendary Colombia winger is still going strong. Cuadrado has always been famous for having pace like a cheetah, but he's also got more tricks than a magician and close control like he's got Super Glue on his boots! Full-backs can't handle his unpredictable changes of speed!

CONFIDENCE	DRIBBLING	TRICKS	AGILITY	WEAK FOOT
90	91	90	78	78

TOP SKILL!
THE CRUYFF TURN!

26 MATCH!

20
RODRYGO

TOP SKILL!
THE REVERSE ELASTICO!

Club: *Real Madrid*
Country: *Brazil*
DOB: *09/01/01*

Rodrygo is the latest Brazilian sensation to swap South America for the bright lights of European football! Real Madrid snapped him up last summer after a series of mind-blowing performances for Santos, but he was loaned back to the Brazilian league until 2019-20 – and now he's ready to show the world his insane dribbling skills!

CONFIDENCE
95

DRIBBLING
98

TRICKS
94

AGILITY
86

WEAK FOOT
76

MATCH! ACADEMY
Play like the stars!

POWERED BY

coerver CoACHING

THE WORLD'S **NO1** SOCCER SKILLS TEACHING METHOD

WWW.COERVER.CO.UK

BERNARDO SILVA
THE U-TURN STEP OVER!

TOTALLY BOSS POSSESSION!

Portugal baller Bernardo Silva uses this epic 1 v 1 move all the time when he's trying to shield the ball from an opponent that's to the side or in front of him. It helps him to retain possession when he's being closely marked!

OPEN UP DEFENCES!

The Man. City megastar performs the U-Turn Step Over when he's looking to create space for a shot or a killer through ball! When Silva does the step over part, he sells the dummy to the defender by making it look like he's going to perform a fast touch away from himself!

THESE SKILLS HELP YOU...

Create chances for yourself and team-mates! ✓

Change direction and shield the ball! ✓

Create space to switch play! ✓

CREATE SPACE!

When Bernardo Silva doesn't have space to run, shoot or pass, he'll use this quality move to shield the ball and change direction quickly. It's perfect for busting out in really tight areas to give you more time and space on the ball. Quality!

IN ASSOCIATION WITH...

adidas

COERVER COACHING

@COERVEREW

TRAINING GROUND!

Now practise the skill yourself!

STEP 1

Take a touch forward with your left foot, then place your right foot on top of the ball to help you quickly change direction!

STEP 2

Step over the ball with your right foot...

STEP 3

...then use the same foot to touch the ball away before accelerating off with your left foot!

NOW WATCH THE VIDEOS!

Go to the MATCH website to see how to do the U-Turn Step Over, plus check out loads more cool ball mastery and mirror move tutorials linked to this epic skill...

U-TURN

FANCY TOE TAPS

www.matchfootball.co.uk

CROSSWORD

Use the clues to fill in MATCH's tricky crossword puzzle!

ACROSS

1. Legendary Bulgaria and Prem skiller, Dimitar _____! (8)

4. Name of the league that Nani's Orlando City compete in! (3)

5. Country that Lorenzo Insigne was born! (5)

8. European country that Dusan Tadic plays for! (6)

9. French megaclub that Man. City signed Bernardo Silva from in 2017! (6)

11. Awesome boot brand that Leo Messi wears! (6)

14. Position that Leroy Sane normally plays! (6)

15. Number of Prem goals that ex-Blues superstar Eden Hazard scored for Chelsea in 2018-19! (7)

16. Shirt number that Paul Pogba usually wears for France! (3)

17. Number of Premier League assists that James Maddison got for Leicester in 2018-19! (5)

18. The foot Mohamed Salah prefers to use! (4)

19. Spain playmaker Isco's real first name! (9)

DOWN

2. Country that Willian was playing in before he joined Chelsea! (6)

3. Number of La Liga titles Thiago Alcantara won at Barcelona! (3)

6. Awesome skill move named after wing wizard Yannick Bolasie! (3,7,5)

7. Angel Di Maria's funny nickname! Clue... think Chinese food! (6)

10. Shirt number that Roberto Firmino wears for Liverpool! (4)

12. Month that PSG and France wonderkid Kylian Mbappe was born! (8)

13. Number of goals that James Rodriguez scored for Colombia at the 2014 World Cup! (3)

14. Prem side Dimitri Payet used to play for! (4,3)

NAME THE COUNTRY!

Have a go at matching the legendary trick machines to the countries they played for!

Romario	Thierry Henry	Faustino Asprilla	Joe Cole	Jay-Jay Okocha	Pavel Nedved
1	2	3	4	5	6

A	B	C	D	E	F
Nigeria	Colombia	Czech Republic	Brazil	England	France

ODD ONE OUT!

Thiago Alcantara

Juan Cuadrado

Angel Di Maria

Nani

Which of these top-quality skillers has never played for a team in La Liga?

Mesut Ozil

Ricardo Quaresma

ANSWERS ON PAGE 60

15
RICARDO QUARESMA

TOP SKILL!
THE TRIVELA!

Club: Kasimpasa
Country: Portugal
DOB: 26/09/83

Quaresma turns 37 in 2020, but he still makes our top 15 for being the king of the trivela! Some critics reckon he does tricks when he doesn't need to, but we love him for it! The iconic Portugal winger loves entertaining fans with his flicks, tricks and eye-popping skills!

CONFIDENCE	DRIBBLING	TRICKS	AGILITY	WEAK FOOT
99	88	98	74	79

14
DOUGLAS COSTA

Club: Juventus
Country: Brazil
DOB: 14/09/90

The Juventus and Brazil trickster bamboozles full-backs with electric dribbling skills. Costa's pace is legendary, but he should be just as famous for beating defenders with unstoppable tricks. The way he nutmegs opponents and sends them sideways with his body swerves is class!

CONFIDENCE	DRIBBLING	TRICKS	AGILITY	WEAK FOOT
88	93	95	88	82

13
DAVID NERES

Club: Ajax
Country: Brazil
DOB: 03/03/97

Neres could be top three in this list in a few years… maybe even No.1 – he's that good! He added goals to his game during Ajax's sensational run to the Champions League semi-finals in 2018-19, but his main impact comes from bossing full-backs with body feints, nutmegs and backheels!

CONFIDENCE	DRIBBLING	TRICKS	AGILITY	WEAK FOOT
91	92	96	90	83

12 KINGSLEY COMAN

Club: Bayern Munich
Country: France
DOB: 13/06/96

We can't believe Bayern Munich don't build their team around Kingsley Coman, because he's an attacking phenomenon! Injuries have slowed down the France wonderkid's career, but he's unstoppable when he's fully fit and on top form. Flip-flaps and stepovers are easy to King Coman!

CONFIDENCE	DRIBBLING	TRICKS	AGILITY	WEAK FOOT
86	96	95	96	80

11 LIONEL MESSI

Club: Barcelona
Country: Argentina
DOB: 24/06/87

Messi has become the ultimate footy star, but people forget he started his career as a tricky wonderkid, full of dribbling skills. His unbeatable mix of speed and close control has been a joy to watch for over 15 years, and hopefully it continues for years to come. A true legend!

CONFIDENCE	DRIBBLING	TRICKS	AGILITY	WEAK FOOT
99	99	89	93	86

TOP SKILL!
FAKE RABONA!

10 KYLIAN MBAPPE

Club: PSG
Country: France
DOB: 20/12/98

The France phenomenon is more than just a lethal goalscorer! When he's not busting nets for fun, Mbappe's terrifying teams across France and Europe with his scary pace and silky skills. Defenders have seen his stepovers over and over again, but they still can't stop them when they face him!

CONFIDENCE	DRIBBLING	TRICKS	AGILITY	WEAK FOOT
99	97	93	99	93

FIFA SKILLS

How many of these super silky moves can you pull off on FIFA?

ONE FOOT SPIN ★★★★

Turn away from defenders in style!

FLICK: R Stick Down, R Stick Left

OR: R Stick Down, R Stick Right

1

2

THREE TOUCH ROULETTE ★★★★

Add a bit of extra flair to the One Foot Spin!

HOLD: L2/LT **+ FLICK:** R Stick Down Left **OR:** R Stick Down Right

1

2

3

STOP & TURN ★★★★

Protect the ball and quickly change direction, before burning away!

FLICK: R Stick Up then R Stick Left

OR: R Stick Up then R Stick Right

BALL HOP ★★★★

Jump into the air with the ball between your feet!

HOLD: L1/LB + **PRESS:** R Stick

RAINBOW ★★★★

Flick the ball over your head - and hopefully your opponent's as well!

FLICK: R Stick Down, R Stick Up + R Stick Up

ANGEL DI MARIA
THE HIGH WAVE!

CREATE SPACE AWAY FROM YOUR MARKER!

Legendary PSG and Argentina wing wizard Angel Di Maria loves using this jaw-dropping stop-start 1 v 1 move to create space away from an opponent that's directly to his side!

Angel di Maria wears adidas® X boots. Find out loads more info at adidas.co.uk/football

SLOW DOWN, THEN ACCELERATE AWAY!

If you're closely marked and don't have space to run, shoot or pass with the ball, use the High Wave 1 v 1 move to slow the defender down, before burning away in the same direction!

THESE SKILLS HELP YOU...

Slow your marker down! ✓

Make space to run with the ball! ✓

Create chances to cross and shoot! ✓

IT'S IDEAL FOR WINGERS!

The High Wave 1 v 1 move is perfect for busting out in wide areas when you're looking to create space to cross the ball into the box, or when moving across goal to have a shot!

IN ASSOCIATION WITH...

adidas | COERVER COACHING

@COERVEREW

TRAINING GROUND!
Now practise the skill yourself!

STEP 1

Take a touch forward, slow down and wave your foot over the ball to make the defender think you're going to step-on with your sole.

STEP 2

Instead, bring your foot back behind the ball.

STEP 3

Push the ball forward with the laces part of your boot and accelerate away. Then repeat with your opposite foot to master the skill with both feet!

NOW WATCH THE VIDEOS!

Go to the MATCH website now to see how to do the High Wave, plus check out loads more cool ball mastery and mirror move tutorials linked to this skill...

SOLE HEEL ROLL | STEP-ON

www.matchfootball.co.uk

9
EDEN HAZARD

Club: *Real Madrid*
Country: *Belgium*
DOB: 07/01/91

Are there any better dribblers in world footy than Eden Hazard on top form? The Belgium wizard shifts direction, busts out chops and hurts defenders with crazy stepovers, all while sprinting at electric speed! He dribbles like he's got Super Glue on his boots and can score flash goals too. What a legend!

CONFIDENCE
98

DRIBBLING
99

TRICKS
93

AGILITY
94

WEAK FOOT
93

TOP SKILL!
THE ELASTICO!

8

OUSMANE DEMBELE

Club: *Barcelona*
Country: *France*
DOB: *15/05/97*

The Barcelona speedster is impossible to stop on top form! Dembele's lightning pace is frightening, but when he mixes it with cool body feints, cut-backs and flashy stepovers, defenders struggle to keep up! The good news is more first-team action with players like Lionel Messi will help him get even better!

CONFIDENCE	DRIBBLING	TRICKS	AGILITY	WEAK FOOT
94	96	94	98	91

7

HAKIM ZIYECH

Club: *Ajax*
Country: *Morocco*
DOB: *19/03/93*

Ajax's young squad shocked the world with some incredible performances in the 2018-19 Champions League, and Ziyech was a massive part of their Hollywood success story. The Morocco trickster mixes mind-boggling close control with clever flicks to keep his opponents guessing!

TOP SKILL!
THE BODY FEINT!

CONFIDENCE	DRIBBLING	TRICKS	AGILITY	WEAK FOOT
96	95	93	92	91

6

VINICIUS JR.

Club: Real Madrid
Country: Brazil
DOB: 12/07/00

The Real Madrid wonderkid looks set for superstardom after an epic first year with the 13-time Champo League winners. Vinicius Jr. mixes eye-popping dribbling skills with the speed of Usain Bolt to make the ultimate winger. His backheels and nutmegs humiliate defenders!

CONFIDENCE	DRIBBLING	TRICKS	AGILITY	WEAK FOOT
93	97	96	97	85

TOP SKILL!
THE FLIP FLAP!

5

JADON SANCHO

TOP SKILL!
THE DRAG BACK!

Club: Borussia Dortmund
Country: England
DOB: 25/03/00

Sancho could be No.1 on this list in a few years, because he baffles defenders with his skills for fun. He could do stepovers and Cruyff turns blindfolded - that's how good he is! Sancho has been ripping up the Bundesliga for Dortmund and now he's ready to shine at Euro 2020 for England!

CONFIDENCE	DRIBBLING	TRICKS	AGILITY	WEAK FOOT
96	96	95	97	91

4

CRISTIANO RONALDO

Club: *Juventus*
Country: *Portugal*
DOB: *05/02/85*

Cristiano Ronaldo is all about goals, goals and more goals nowadays, but he still busts out loads of awesome tricks when he needs to. Ron started his career as a flashy winger, and looked like he was trying to break the world record for most stepovers in a game during his time at Sporting and Man. United. Legend!

TOP SKILL!
RONALDO CHOP!

CONFIDENCE
99

DRIBBLING
94

TRICKS
93

AGILITY
88

WEAK FOOT
99

DID YOU KNOW?

BEFORE JOINING JUVENTUS IN 2018, CR7 BECAME REAL MADRID'S ALL-TIME TOP SCORER WITH 450 GOALS IN JUST 438 GAMES!

BRAIN-BUSTER!

How well do you know some of footy's best tricksters?

1. True or False? Neymar made his pro debut for the same Brazilian club as footy legend Ronaldinho!

2. Which Italian team did Xherdan Shaqiri play for before joining the Premier League?

3. How many caps has wing wizard Douglas Costa won for Brazil – more or less than 30?

4. How many goals did David Neres score for Ajax against Real Madrid in the 2018-19 Champions League?

5. Name the awesome boot brand that speedster Sadio Mane wears!

6. Which African country does Samuel Chukwueze play for – Nigeria or Cameroon?

7. How old was Kai Havertz when he made his Bundesliga debut for Bayer Leverkusen in 2016?

8. Who was Real Madrid new boy Rodrygo's footy idol growing up – Gareth Bale or Eden Hazard?

9. How much did Barcelona pay to sign Frenkie de Jong from Ajax – more or less than £60 million?

10. Hatem Ben Arfa has played for two English clubs during his career – Hull and who else?

1...
2...
3...
4...
5...
6...
7...
8...
9...
10..

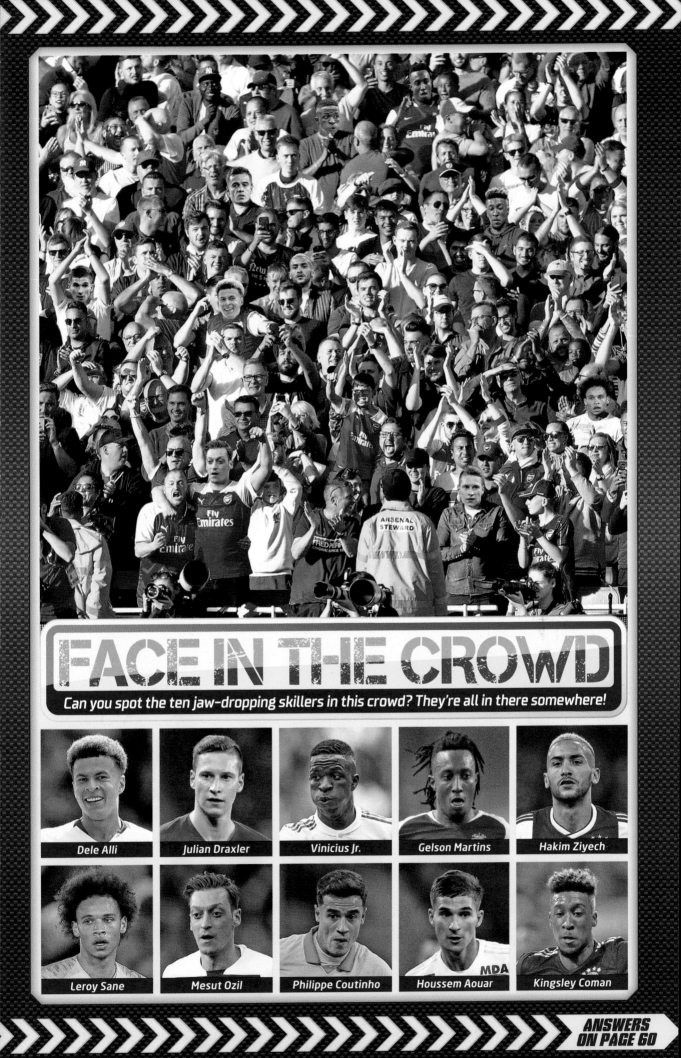

FACE IN THE CROWD

Can you spot the ten jaw-dropping skillers in this crowd? They're all in there somewhere!

Dele Alli

Julian Draxler

Vinicius Jr.

Gelson Martins

Hakim Ziyech

Leroy Sane

Mesut Ozil

Philippe Coutinho

Houssem Aouar

Kingsley Coman

ANSWERS ON PAGE 60

FIFA SKILLS

Impress your mates by busting out these sick tricks on FIFA!

SOUL TRAP ★ + FLAIR TRAIT

As the ball is bouncing in front of you, use this mega sweet move!

HOLD: L2/LT | **+ FLICK:** R Stick Up

1

2

BALL ROLL FLICK ★★★★★

Your opponent won't know which way to look!

| **FLICK:** R Stick Right | **PUSH:** R Stick | **OR FLICK:** R Stick Left | **PUSH:** R Stick |

1

2

JUGGLING ★

Simply get the ball up in the air by juggling it... well simple!

HOLD: L2/LT

L2 / LT

TAP: R1/RB

R1 / RB

1

2

AROUND THE WORLD
★★★★★

Go for this piece of jaw-dropping showboating while juggling!

ROTATE:
R Stick
Up, Right,
Down, Left

OR:
R Stick
Down, Left,
Up, Right

R ↱↲   R ↵↱

1

2

SOMBRERO FLICK
★★★★★

Or you can lift the ball up and flick it back over your head. Well flash!

JUGGLE & HOLD: L Stick down

L ↓

1

2

OPEN UP FAKE ★

Open out your player's body as if going for a finesse shot, then fake!

HOLD: L1/LB

L1 / LB

TAP: Circle/B + Cross/A

● / ● + X / A

1

2

3

RIYAD MAHREZ

Club: Man. City
Country: Algeria
DOB: 21/02/91

If you love players who rock at close control and dribble out of danger with ease, Mahrez is as good as it gets. His unique dribbling technique and slick tricks were a major factor behind Leicester's shock Prem title win in 2015-16, then he moved on to Man. City to dazzle a new set of fans!

CONFIDENCE 96

DRIBBLING 99

TRICKS 96

AGILITY 97

WEAK FOOT 91

DID YOU KNOW?

MAHREZ WAS HIS COUNTRY'S JOINT-TOP SCORER AS HE FIRED ALGERIA TO GLORY AT THE 2019 AFRICA CUP OF NATIONS!

2

WILFRIED ZAHA

TOP SKILL!
THE HOCUS POCUS!

Club: Crystal Palace
Country: Cote d'Ivoire
DOB: 10/11/92

Zaha picks up the silver medal in our list after another year of mind-boggling skills in the Premier League. Opposition managers always put loads of focus on stopping Zaha with man-to-man marking or multiple players sticking to him like glue, but Zaha has the skills in his locker to escape without any problems!

DID YOU KNOW?
ZAHA WON TWO INTERNATIONAL CAPS FOR ENGLAND, BEFORE SWITCHING ALLEGIANCES TO COTE D'IVOIRE BACK IN 2017!

CONFIDENCE
97

DRIBBLING
98

TRICKS
97

AGILITY
94

WEAK FOOT
86

1
NEYMAR

Club: *PSG*
Country: *Brazil*
DOB: *5/02/92*

Neymar is our No.1 for the second year in a row! We tried to find a flashier footy star, but it was mission impossible, because Neymar is just on a different level! The Brazil icon mixes insane dribbling with jaw-dropping skills to make the ultimate trick king. Who else tries rainbow flicks in real games? Neymar is next level!

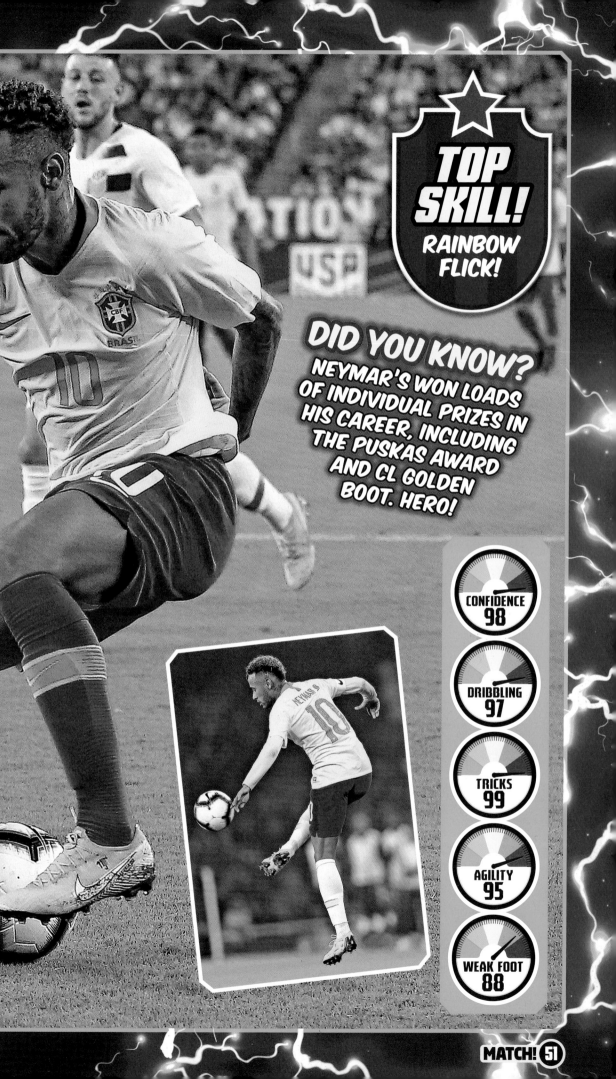

TOP SKILL!
RAINBOW FLICK!

DID YOU KNOW?
NEYMAR'S WON LOADS OF INDIVIDUAL PRIZES IN HIS CAREER, INCLUDING THE PUSKAS AWARD AND CL GOLDEN BOOT. HERO!

CONFIDENCE
98

DRIBBLING
97

TRICKS
99

AGILITY
95

WEAK FOOT
88

STAT ATTACK!

NEYMAR

Neymar tops our list once again as the No.1 trick machine on the planet, so get a load of some of the coolest stats from his epic career!

5
Neymar won five trophies in his first two seasons with PSG, including two Ligue 1 titles. Epic!

198
He joined PSG from Barcelona for a world-record £198 million in 2017. Wowzers!

49
Neymar was destroying defenders in Brazil, before Barcelona paid Santos £49 million to sign him in 2013!

8
He won eight trophies during his spell at Barça, including the Champions League, Club World Cup and two La Liga titles!

2014
He was the poster boy as Brazil hosted the 2014 World Cup, but was injured for the shock 7-1 semi-final defeat to Germany!

6
The legendary dribbler has scored six World Cup goals, including doubles against Cameroon and Croatia at the 2014 tournament!

2015

Neymar won the Champions League with Barcelona in 2014-15, scoring in the final against Juventus, and was the joint-top scorer with ten goals!

34

The Brazil trickster hit 34 goals in just 37 Ligue 1 games in his first two seasons at PSG!

68

Neymar scored 68 goals in 123 La Liga games during his time at Barcelona!

1

He scored the winning penalty as hosts Brazil won the 2016 Summer Olympics – their first ever football gold medal!

4

Neymar scored four goals and was voted the tournament's best player as Brazil won the 2013 Confederations Cup!

MATCH! ACADEMY
Play like the stars!

ROBERTO FIRMINO
PULL SPIN STEP OVER!

PROTECT THE BALL!

The Pull Spin Step Over 1 v 1 move is perfect for shielding the ball from an opponent who's closing you down from the side or in front. Awesome Liverpool finisher Roberto Firmino uses it when he's leading the line for The Reds. He's a proper baller!

BUST OUT IN ATTACKING AREAS!

Because Firmino often plays through the middle, he uses this 1 v 1 move in the final third of the pitch when he's looking to create space to run, play a killer pass or have a shot at goal. The Brazilian magician is a real expert at it!

Roberto Firmino wears adidas® Nemeziz boots.
Find out loads more at adidas.co.uk/football

THESE SKILLS HELP YOU...

Boss opponents 1 v 1 to the side or in front of you! ✓

Create more assists and goal chances! ✓

Shield the ball from your marker! ✓

ACCELERATE PAST YOUR MARKER!

This epic 1 v 1 move is great for beating your marker! Roberto takes a diagonal touch away from the space he wants to run into. This helps move the defender, before doing the Pull Spin Step Over to run into the space he's created!

IN ASSOCIATION WITH...

adidas | coerver COACHING

@COERVEREW

Turn over now to book your FREE Coerver® Performance Academy training session!

TRAINING GROUND!
Now practise the skill yourself!

STEP 1

Push the ball forward with your left foot, reach with your right foot and pull the ball back.

STEP 2

Spin around to your left, pulling the ball back with your left foot as you do so.

STEP 3

Step over the ball with your right foot, spin right with the outside of the same foot, then accelerate away with your left foot!

NOW WATCH THE VIDEOS!

Go to the MATCH website now to see how to do the Pull Spin Step Over, plus check out loads more cool ball mastery and 1 v 1 mirror move videos linked to this skill...

PULL SPIN

PULL SPIN 360

www.matchfootball.co.uk

COMPETITION

PICK YOUR TOP 5 TRICK KINGS!

WIN A MATCH! SUBSCRIPTION!

You've seen our list of the top 50 skillers on the planet – now choose your own top five for the chance to win an epic prize!

Just photocopy this page, list your five favourite footy tricksters, fill out your details and send it to MATCH! One lucky winner will then be picked at random to win a year's free subscription to the best footy magazine on the planet – MATCH!

Post your entry to: Football Skills 2020, MATCH Magazine, Kelsey Media, Regent House, Welbeck Way, Peterborough, Cambridgeshire, PE2 7WH
Closing date: January 31, 2020.

1.

2.

3.

4.

5.

NAME:

DATE OF BIRTH:

ADDRESS:

MOBILE:

EMAIL:

Wordfit — P20

KAKA
MEAZZA • PUSKAS
PROSINECKI
MARADONA
GARRINCHA
DICANIO
PELE • RONALDO
DENILSON
CANTONA
KLINSMANN / KAMPRG
WADDLE
GINOLA • ROBINHO
CRUYFF • ZOLA • OKOCHA • BEST
ORTEGA
FIGO • EUSEBIO

Richarlison Quiz — P21

1. Shorter than six foot;
2. Fluminense; 3. More than
£30 million; 4. El Salvador;
5. False - his full name is
Richarlison de Andrade.

Spot The Ball — P21

G10.

Name The Country — P31

1. Romario – D. Brazil;
2. Thierry Henry – F. France;
3. Faustino Asprilla – B. Colombia;
4. Joe Cole – E. England;
5. Jay-Jay Okocha – A. Nigeria;
6. Pavel Nedved – C. Czech Rep.

Odd One Out — P31

Juan Cuadrado.

Crossword — P30

BERBATOV
RUSSIA
MLS
ITALY
SERBIA • MONACO
ADIDAS • WINGER
SIXTEEN
SIX • SEVEN
LEFT
WEST HAM
FRANCISCO

Face In The Crowd — P45

Brain-Buster — P44

1. False; 2. Inter; 3. More than
30; 4. One; 5. New Balance;
6. Nigeria; 7. 17 years old;
8. Eden Hazard; 9. More than
£60 million; 10. Newcastle.

Wordsearch — P58

WORDSEARCH
Find 30 trick machines that just missed out on our top 50!

(FODEN, PERISIC, MARCELO, JANUZAJ, SANCHEZ...)

Footy Mis-Match — P59